RESTORING THE BRIDE

GW00467740

Anne Simpson-Phillipson

2009

First Edition

Published and Printed by

Leiston Press
Masterlord Industrial Estate
Leiston
Suffolk
IP16 4JD
Telephone Number: 01728 833003
Email: glenn@leistonpress.com

ISBN 978-0-9562896-4-3

CONTENTS

INTRODUCTION - The Vision of the Hour concerning the Bride of Christ

CHAPTER 1 - ANCIENT JEWISH WEDDING CUSTOMS
Includes:-
> The choosing of the bride. The bride price.
> The bride's acceptance. The engagement including;
> The cup of the covenant, The ketubah, gifts for the
> bride, the mikvah, the betrothal vow, and the
> bridegroom departing.

CHAPTER 2 - THE BRIDE WAITS AND MAKES
                    HERSELF READY
Includes:-
> The preparation of the bride. Our task before the Lord's
> return.
> The signs of the times, and the warrior bride.

CHAPTER 3 - THE BRIDEGROOM RETURNS
Includes:-
> The rapture of the church, and why I believe the church
> must leave before the tribulation and concluding with
> the wedding supper of the lamb.

INTRODUCTION

I believe that the message of restoring the bride is God's prophetic word for this hour and this book is the result of the Lord's revelation to me recently concerning that hour that I believe that we are living in right now. I believe that we are living in the hour when the Lord is preparing and restoring his people in preparation for his return and he is bringing a fresh revelation concerning who the bride of Christ is. Throughout this book we will be looking at some of the ancient Jewish wedding customs and seeing how these relate to the things that Jesus spoke to his disciples and how they relate to us today. We will see amazing similarities between what took place in a Jewish wedding and the things that Jesus did and said.

Revelation 22 v 17 "The Spirit and the bride say come".

The Bible refers to the body of Christ as being the bride of Christ and the passage in revelation is the Holy Spirit and the bride calling for the Lord to return to take us home to be with him. I believe that the Lord is returning soon to take his people home and that this is the hour when he is bringing this revelation to the church and calling us to be ready.

The Bible declares in 1 Thessalonians 4 v 16 :-

"For the Lord himself will come down from heaven with a loud command, with the voice of the archangel and with the trumpet call of God"

When the Lord returns to take his people home - there will be a trumpet call from God. The Lord revealed to me, that we are now living prophetically in the hour of the pre-trumpet call. This is the time when the Lord is giving his people a time of grace and favour in which to prepare themselves for the return of the Lord.

The Bible says that Jesus is coming back for a pure and spotless bride without stain or wrinkle, a holy people set apart for him. This is therefore the time when the Lord is restoring his people and preparing them for his return.

I believe that ministry-wise we are also living in the hour of the John the Baptist anointing.

Luke 3 v 4 " A voice of one calling in the desert, prepare the way for the Lord"

John preached a message of repentance for the people in preparation for the first coming of the Lord. I believe that what we are seeing now and what the Lord is calling his people to preach more and more now is the message of repentance and preparation for the second coming of the Lord.

As the Lord began to show me the bride, I realised that half of the bride was missing, half of the bride was asleep and half of the bride was battered and bruised and in need of healing. There are some people who the Lord has chosen to be a part of his bride who are yet to come into a knowledge of the Lord. This is the final hour when the Lord is calling people unto himself like never before and we are the voice calling in the wilderness, declaring the gospel to the world. For those who have received the Lord and are a part of the bride, a lot of them have gone to sleep and are not expecting and ready for the return of the Lord. God is sounding the trumpet for us to wake up and prepare ourselves for what is about to take place. The other part of the bride is hurting and instead of being a glorious radiant bride, they have become a dull and lifeless bride. Many times the circumstances of life have taken away the radiance that the Lord intends us to have. I believe that this is the hour when the Lord is restoring and healing and bringing back the true radiance to his bride. When Moses was with the Lord for 40 days, the Bible says that his face shone with the radiance of the glory of God. Everyone who saw him, saw the glory of God on his face. People need to be able to see the radiance of the glory of God on our faces. The Lord is going to pour out his Spirit in these last days in such an amazing way, bringing back the radiance to the faces of his people.

Isaiah 60 v 1 "Arise shine for your light has come and the glory of the Lord rises upon you. See darkness covers the earth and thick darkness is over the peoples, but the Lord rises upon you and his glory appears over you"

As the world in which we live gets darker, then God's intention is that his people will shine brighter than ever before and stand out in the midst of the darkness. When the earth is at the darkest that the Lord will allow it to be and the church is at the brightest that it can be, then the Lord will return to collect his bride with the trumpet call and the shout from heaven. Until then, we have work to do to bring forth the light and glory of God into the earth.

No-one knows exactly on what day the Lord will return as it says in Mathew 24 v 36-38 only the Father in heaven. In fact for the people who do not have any concept of the Lord's return, it will be a day not unlike any other day. People will be eating and drinking and getting married - in other words, they will have no idea that their lives are about to change forever when the Lord returns to collect his people but he will leave behind those who don't know him. It will be a day like no other day in history - can you imagine the news on that day when a great number of the population have disappeared?!

Mathew 24 v 40 "Two men will be in the field, one will be taken and the other left"

The question that each one of us must ask ourselves is this:- are we sure that we will be taken by the Lord or is there a possibility that we may get left behind? After the Lord has taken his people, there will be 7 years of tribulation that will come upon the earth, such as the world has never seen before. We look around the world today and see many disasters and horrors and yet that will be mild compared to the tribulation to come on those left behind. God is sounding the pre-trumpet call now, warning us to get ready, to put our lives in order, so that when the final trumpet call sounds, we will be ready to meet our Lord in the air.

Further in the book we will look at ways that we can discern the hour that we are living in and how we can see that the time is short and that we need to be wise in the way that we live our lives.

In order for us to be able to understand about the concept of the body of Christ being the bride, we need to have an understanding of what took place in ancient biblical weddings. We will see through this teaching how a lot of the things that Jesus spoke was referring to him being the bridegroom and us being the bride. This message is often easier understood by women than by men, but in fact we are all the bride of Christ - men and women, for in Christ we are Spirit not flesh. Many times throughout the Bible the Lord refers to himself as our husband:-

Isaiah 62 v 5 "As a bridegroom rejoices over his bride, so will God rejoice over you"
Isaiah 54 v 5 "For your maker is your husband - the Lord Almighty is his name"

God spoke to his chosen people Israel and referred to himself as their bridegroom. Through the cross, both Jew and gentile have been brought into the covenant with the Lord and all who will receive Jesus are gathered in to be a part of the bride of Christ with Jesus as our bridegroom. The one who cares and nurtures us, protects and provides for us, the perfect bridegroom. The image of being a bride is one of intimacy and one of being cared for. The Lord wants a close relationship with his people; he wants to draw us closer to himself and to be our provider. Many times throughout the scriptures, we see that time after time the people went after other gods and committed spiritual adultery by forsaking the Lord. Many times they found themselves in trouble and had to cry out to God for forgiveness. Each time he restored them and gathered them back to himself again. At the cross, he made an everlasting covenant with us to offer us total forgiveness and restoration. When we think about a marriage, it will conjure up different emotions for each person. For some, it will be a pleasant experience, for some it will bring back memories of disappointment or abuse or bereavement. I believe that no matter what our experiences of an earthly marriage, God wants to show us the picture of a perfect marriage - the marriage between him and the church. God intended that marriage on earth would be a picture of the marriage in heaven; however because of sin entering into the world, earthly marriages have been stained by that sin and are not the perfect picture that the Lord intended them to be. He is bringing revelation to the church at this time, of his love towards his bride and wants to restore the image of heavenly marriage as he intended it to be. I believe that for some people this move of God will bring a great release of healing for those who have been hurt by earthly marriages as the Lord begins to reveal what true love and care really is and should be.

Ephesians 5 v 32 "This is a profound mystery, but I am talking about Christ and the church"

The bible refers to earthly marriage as being an example of the true marriage of heaven, but calls it a mystery as it is so difficult to understand except through spiritual revelation. Heavenly marriage is a spiritual union between Christ and the church. That is why the bible says that there will be no marriage as we now understand it in heaven because we will all be married to the Lord.

Mathew 22 v 30 "At the resurrection, people will neither marry nor be given in marriage; they will be like the angels in heaven"

Some people find this hard to understand as we can only think of our relationships as we know them here on earth. I do believe that we will still know who our loved ones are but the relationships that we will have with them in heaven will be different from what they are now on earth. Our minds now can only think in earthly terms, but one day we will know all things from a spiritual mind-set.

I want us to now look at what would happen in an ancient Jewish wedding so that we can understand the parallels that Jesus was making to us being his bride.

CHAPTER 1

ANCIENT JEWISH WEDDING CUSTOMS

The Bride is Chosen

In ancient Israel the father of the bridegroom would choose a bride for his son and would often send his trusted servant to find a suitable bride for his Son. In the story of Genesis 24 we see Abraham sending his servant to get a wife for his son Isaac.

By the time of Jesus, it was acceptable for the bridegroom to go to the bride's house himself in order to ask for her hand in marriage. Unlike in today's culture, where it is quite acceptable for a woman to choose and go after a man, this was not the case in Jesus' time on earth. Only by understanding the customs of the time, can we fully understand the concept of the bride of Christ. It is a wonderful feeling to be chosen! It makes us feel special, that someone has chosen us. I am sure that we can think back to our school days, when maybe people were being chosen for a sports team and we stood there waiting to see if we would be chosen and can remember how pleased we were when someone said that they wanted us in their team. I am sure that we can also think of times, when we were left standing till the end and no-one had chosen us! And we had to just go in whatever team was left but were left feeling that no-one had really wanted us on their team. I believe that the greatest need inside each one of us is to feel wanted and chosen.

The wonderful image of the bridegroom choosing a bride is that God chose us because he thinks that we are special and very precious to him.

Ephesians 1 v 4-5 "For God chose us in him before the creation of the world to be holy and blameless in his sight. In love he predestined us to be adopted as his sons through Jesus Christ"

This is an amazing scripture that tells us that even before the creation of the world, God knew all about YOU! and he chose you to be holy and blameless and to be adopted into his family. Some people grow up feeling that they were not really wanted by their natural family, maybe they were even told that they were a mistake and were not supposed to be here and yet God says that he chose you before the creation of the world. There is a God in heaven who thinks that you are so special, that even while he was flinging stars into space and creating the sun and the moon, he was thinking about you and about how special you are.

John 15 v 16 "You did not choose me, but I chose you"

We often think that we decided to choose the Lord at some point in our lives, but the truth is that God had already chosen us and set us apart to know him. He was just waiting until the day when he knew in his foreknowledge that we would accept him. You may ask, if God chooses some people to be set apart, does that mean that he does not choose some people? and is that fair that God chooses some and not others?

I believe that the answer to this is, that God has foreknowledge of all things and even knows the decisions that we will make in our life. I believe that he therefore chooses us because he knows that we will one day accept him. It is not a case of God choosing one person more than another but simply that he knows who will accept him and who will reject him and so he chooses those who he knows will accept him. Jesus said that many are invited but few are chosen, because he chooses according to his fore-knowledge. He invites all, because he desires that all would come, but not everyone will accept his invitation. Therefore he only chooses those, who he knows will choose him.

In the illustrations from both old and modern customs we see a picture of the Lord coming to choose us for his bride.

Just as the Father would choose a suitable bride for his Son, so the Father in heaven has chosen us to be the bride for his son. We then see Jesus leaving his Fathers house in heaven and coming to our home on earth in order to purchase us as his bride. He loved us so much that he was willing to leave the comfort of heaven and come to earth to make us his bride.

We also see the Holy Spirit acting as the servant on behalf of the Father who is now here on earth and drawing us to Jesus to be his bride.

John 15 v 26 "but when the counsellor comes, he will testify about me"

Jesus said that the Holy Spirit would speak to us about him and draw us unto him. That is part of the job of the Holy Spirit, to draw all men to Jesus. One day when the bride is fully prepared, the Holy Spirit will escort us back to the Father's house to be with the Son. Right now, the Father is in heaven, Jesus is in heaven preparing the wedding room but the Holy Spirit has been left here on earth to draw forth and prepare the bride.

The Price was paid

In biblical times and indeed still in some cultures even today there is a price to be paid for a bride, called a bride price. Bringing up a daughter was an expensive business as she was not able to work in the same way as a man and would not carry on the family name; therefore it was necessary for the family to be compensated for giving their daughter in marriage. It was also a sign to both the bride and her family of how much the bridegroom loved and valued his daughter that he was willing to pay a high price for her. That which you pay a high price for, you value and look after more carefully. If we only pay a cheap price for something then it can be discarded and another bought, but if we pay a high price for something, then we look after what we have bought. The bridegroom would give costly gifts to the family of the bride that he wished to marry. This could be in many different ways, including gold, silver, animals, clothes, jewellery etc, but a price would be agreed upon and paid to the family of the bride.

Genesis 24 v 52 "When Abraham's servant heard what they said, he bowed down to the ground before the Lord. Then the servant brought out gold and silver, jewellery and articles of clothing and gave them to Rebekah, he also gave costly gifts to her brother and her mother"

We see that when Abraham's servant realised that his mission to find a wife for Isaac was successful, he then proceeded to bring out the costly gifts that he had been given to bring with him. Another example that we see of a price being paid is in the story in Genesis 29 where Jacob agrees to work for Laban for 7 years in exchange for his daughter Rachel's hand in marriage.

1 Peter 1 v 18 "For you know that it was not with perishable things such as silver or gold that you were redeemed from your empty way of life, but with the precious blood of Christ"

Jesus paid a price for his bride that is higher than anyone has ever paid before, so great was his love for us and so great was his determination to make us his bride that he paid for us with his own blood. Jesus even paid the price for us before he even knew that we would accept him. How many of us would pay for something expensive without any guarantee that we were going to receive what we had purchased? Jesus demonstrated to us that he is the perfect bridegroom - he was willing to sign a contract in his own blood before we had even accepted him.

Romans 5 v 8 "But God demonstrates his own love for us in this, while we were still sinners Christ died for us"

Many of us may have received many lovely gifts and presents from people that we loved at different times in our lives but very few of us could say that someone gave their life for us.

The bridegroom would pay a bride price - Jesus paid his bride price - it was called the cross.

Hosea

The story of Hosea is a wonderful example of how God searches out for his lost bride in order to restore her to himself. In the story of Hosea the prophet, we see that he was asked by the Lord to go and marry someone who the Lord knew would be unfaithful to him. This may seem like a strange request for the Lord to ask of someone, but he was using Hosea to give a picture to the people of Israel of their backsliding away from him. I often feel sorry for some of the Old Testament prophets as often they had to do many strange and sacrificial things in order to paint a picture to the people of the time. In this instance Hosea is asked to marry Gomer who he knows will break his heart and go off with other men. After Gomer has left and gone off with other men and abandoned Hosea, the Lord speaks to him to go and find his wayward wife and bring her back. When Hosea goes to find his un-faithful wife, he finds her at a slave market and he has to pay money to purchase back his own wife.

Hosea 3 v 2 "So I bought her for fifteen shekels of silver and about a homer and a lethek of barley".

Hosea had to pay money to purchase back his un-faithful wife.

This is a beautiful picture of Christ and the church. We belonged to the Lord all along, but chose to go our own way and ended up in the slavery of our own sin, but because of the extent of God's love for us, he did not leave us where we deserved to be. He came and paid the price to bring us back to a place of intimacy and restoration with him.

The Bride must accept

Just because the bridegroom would choose a bride and go to her house to pursue her, did not mean that she was under obligation to accept. It was not a case of her not having a say in the matter, she needed to accept his proposal of marriage to her. In the same way, The Lord holds out his hand to us but he will never force us to accept him, we must come to him of our own free choice.

In the story of Abraham's servant going to find a wife for his son Isaac, we see that Rebekah was asked by her family if she wished to go with the man - Genesis 24 v 58 "They called Rebekah and asked her - will you go with this man?"

A bridegroom would often go to the house of the woman that he wanted to marry and knock on the door, if she answered the door; she was indicating her acceptance towards him.

Jesus said in Revelation 3 v 20 "Behold I stand at the door and knock, if anyone hears my voice and opens the door, I will come in and eat with him"

Jesus stands knocking at the door to our hearts and he wants us to open the door to let him into our lives and allow him to be our bridegroom, but he will never force his way into our lives. He is a gentleman and wants us to come to him in freedom of choice and because we desire to be with him not because we are forced to accept him. When we force someone to be with us, they will never love us in a correct way and the Lord wants our unconditional love not a coerced love.

John 1 v 12 "But to all who received him, he gave the right to become children of God"

God desires that all would come, but we have a choice to make.

<u>A betrothal or engagement would take place</u>

When the bride gave her acceptance of the marriage, there would be an engagement as we would call it or as it would have been called then - a betrothal. Again we need to understand about the times and cultures of the day in order to get a better understanding of the spiritual significance for us. In our culture, it is possible to get engaged to someone and to then break off that engagement some time later without anyone thinking anything bad of us - sometimes we can be engaged several times to different people before deciding to marry someone. However in this culture a betrothal was as binding as a marriage itself and was taken very seriously indeed. A written contract would be signed and could only be nullified by an official divorce. The couple were married in every sense of the word apart from the physical union which would take place at the final wedding, but legally they were married after the betrothal. That is why when Joseph was pledged to be married to Mary and she was found to be with child the scripture says that:-

Mathew 1 v 19 "but because Joseph was a righteous man and did not want to expose her to public disgrace, he had in mind to divorce her quietly"

Mary was found to be with child supernaturally by the Holy Spirit, but Joseph could not understand this and was going to divorce his bride until an angel of the Lord appeared to him and confirmed that indeed the baby was from the Holy Spirit. We often forget what an amazing sacrifice Mary and Joseph gave to bring Jesus into the world, as the world around them at that time would have frowned upon a baby born out of wedlock and Mary could have even been stoned to death. For her to explain that the baby was not conceived naturally would have been very hard for people to understand.

From this story though we can see that being betrothed was as legally binding as a marriage and to get out of a betrothal would take a divorce.

In light of this, we can see that we are engaged to the Lord just waiting for the final wedding supper to take place on that great day of the Lord. At the moment we have been given the Holy Spirit as a guarantee of what is to come. It is a poor illustration but the Holy Spirit is like an engagement ring that has been given to us. The difference being that the Lord does not break off engagements and nor does he divorce his people. We can therefore be assured that our relationship with Jesus is secure forever.

Ephesians 1 v 13 "Having believed, you were marked in him with a seal, the promised Holy Spirit who is a deposit guaranteeing our inheritance until the redemption of those who are God's possession - to the praise of his glory"

The Lord has given us the Holy Spirit as the deposit of the marriage to him one day. The Spirit of God within us is the one who testifies with our spirit that we truly are the children of God.

After the betrothal, a trumpet would sound as a sign of the couple's engagement to one another. The next trumpet would sound on the wedding day. We are living in the time of the first trumpet call and waiting for the second trumpet call.

Ketubah

As part of the betrothal there would be a ketubah which was a written contract between the couple. The bridegroom would give many promises to the bride that he would provide for her and take care of her and nurture her etc. This ketubah would be signed by at least two witnesses and sealed and be given to the bride to keep. The bride would value this contract highly and would keep it in a place of safety.

We have also been given a contract along with our betrothal to the Lord. His word is his promise to us, he has promised to provide for us, to look after us, to care and nurture us and he has promised to one day return for us. The two witnesses to our betrothal to Jesus are the Father and the Holy Spirit. It is also interesting that in Revelation during the time of the tribulation, God will have two witnesses on the earth. (Rev 11). In Deuteronomy 17 v 6 concerning the laws of the time, God said that everything must be established by two or three witnesses and that a claim was not valid if there was only one witness. Therefore for a wedding vow, the Lord will establish it with at least two witnesses. Every time we read his word, we are reading his promise to us. Do we value his word in our lives just like the bride valued her ketubah?

The bride would feel secure in the promises of the Ketubah that the bridegroom would take care of her and provide for everything that she needed. She was preparing to leave the security of her father's house and the responsibility for her welfare was being handed over to her future husband. The bridegroom would therefore make a contract stating his intentions towards her.

When we read the covenant of the word of God given to us by the Lord, we can feel secure that he has made provision for us to be taken care of. We can read any promise in the word and can claim it as rightfully ours in Christ because we are the bride.

Psalm 23 "The Lord is my shepherd I shall not be in want"

Jesus is the true shepherd who promises to take care of his sheep, to lead us beside still waters, to restore our soul, to lead us in paths of righteousness. He has promised to protect us from the evil and to vindicate us in the presence of our enemies. A true bridegroom would never let his bride be attacked or hurt in any way, he would protect her. In the same way we can rest assured that Jesus looks after us and cares for us in every way. He has promised so much to us in his word including not only forgiveness but also healing and restoration and provision. He has promised to lead us and guide us in good pathways and to go before us in this life. The bride would treasure all the promises from her bridegroom while she was awaiting his return. We also should treasure God's words and promises to us while we await his return. There is a scripture that says that we perish because of a lack of knowledge (Hosea 4 v 6). God has made so many promises to us in his word, but unless we read his word to find out what provision he has made for us, we can often miss out on the blessings that he has for us. When we are ignorant of his promises, we can be robbed of them. When we do not realise that provision was made for our healing on the cross, then we will not seek for healing. When we do not realise that God wants us to prosper, then we will be content to live in lack. When we do not realise that God has a perfect plan for our lives, then we will be content to live an aimless life without purpose. The bible is our ketubah! We need to read what God has promised us, so that we can begin to experience everything that he has purchased for us.

2 Corinthians 1 v 20 "For no matter how many promises God has made, they are Yes in Christ and so through him the Amen is spoken to the glory of God"

We can look through the word of God and every promise that God made, is for us in Christ. Let's look at a few examples of the promises of God and see all that God has promised to us his bride.

Our Ketubah from God

Healing

Exodus 15 v 26 "I am the Lord who heals you"
God declared himself as a healing God right back in the Old Testament and then we also see that in:-
Isaiah 53 v 5 "By his stripes we are healed"

One of the promises that God has made towards his people is that he will heal us. He has always been a healing God and he does not change. At the cross, he took not only our sins but also our sicknesses and by his wounds we are healed. When Jesus walked on the earth, he also demonstrated the will of the Father when he went around everywhere healing the sick and also giving power and authority to his disciples to do the same thing. When we are sick, we can look at our ketubah and see that Jesus has promised us healing. He does not want his bride to be sick and in pain, he wants us to be healthy. There can be many different reasons why people get sick and sometimes we may need to change our lifestyles etc, but ultimately God's intention is that we walk in health.

Victory

Another promise that God gives towards his people, is the ability to walk in victory in our lives. Romans 5 v 17 says that we shall rule and reign in life and 2 Corinthians 2 v 14 says that God will always cause us to triumph. We may go through different trials and situations in our lives and we are not exempt from them, however God's promise to us is that we can come through them and out of them victorious. No matter what situation we may be going through, God can take a hold of that situation and turn it around for his glory and bring good out of it. The promise of God to us is that we can emerge victorious from any situation that we may face. We can come out of it stronger and with greater authority than before we went into it. I love the story in Daniel, where Shadrach, Meshach and Abednego were put into the fire for refusing to bow down to the golden image that Nebuchadnezzar had set up. When they were thrown into the fire, the King's servants are amazed to see that a fourth person had appeared in the fire and that the 3 men were un-bound and un-harmed. When the three men were ordered out of the fire, there was no smell of fire on them and the King was so impressed that he ordered that they should be promoted, instead of killed. The fire that was supposed to kill them actually ended up promoting them. The enemy may send many things into our lives to try to destroy us, but God has promised to walk through the fire with us and if we will hand all our circumstances to the Lord, then he can bring us out of the fire with no smell of fire on us, and promote us for his purposes.

Freedom

The Lord also promises that we shall walk in freedom in our lives

2 Corinthians 3 v 17 "now where the Spirit of the Lord is, there is freedom"

God does not want us to be bound by different circumstances of life; we are a people purchased to live in freedom. Free to be who God created us to be, free from the labels of the past, from the mistakes of the past. Jesus took all our sins and mistakes at the cross, so that we can walk in freedom. He promises us not only physical healing but emotional healing and wholeness. Jesus said that his yoke was easy and light, we do not need to walk with a heavy yoke over our lives, we have been set free.

Galatians 5 v 1 "It is for freedom that Christ has set us free. Stand firm then and do not let yourselves be burdened again by a yoke of slavery"

We can be in bondage to many different things in our lives, but Jesus came to set the captives free.

Guidance

John 10 v 27 "My sheep listen to my voice; I know them and they follow me"

Jesus gave the illustration of being a good shepherd who takes care of his sheep. As our husband, the Lord is responsible for directing us and guiding us in the way that we should go in our lives. Because of the Lord's foreknowledge of what is ahead, he is able to lead us into the right pathways and we do not need to have any fear of following him, because he knows what is ahead and has already been there to prepare the way for us.

Provision

The Lord has also promised to provide for us - 1 Timothy 6 v 17 "God, who richly provides us with everything for our enjoyment". Proverbs 10 v 22 "The blessing of the Lord brings wealth and he adds no trouble to it".

God has promised in his word to provide for us, not only for our basic needs, but also for our enjoyment as well. Jesus came that we might have life and have it abundantly; therefore I believe that God wants us to enjoy life! A lot of things that are enjoyable can be free, but also a lot of things in this life also cost money, so it is a fact of living on earth that we need money. Proverbs tells us that the blessing of the Lord will bring wealth without trouble. A lot of people who have money also have trouble as well, but the Lord has promised that he will bless us financially without adding any trouble to it. A lot of people don't think that Christians should ask the Lord for material possessions, but the bible is full of people who were blessed financially and as long as our heart is towards God and not things then he will add things to us. We may not all become millionaires but he does desire for us to not be in want. A proper bridegroom would provide financially for his bride, so if Jesus is our bridegroom, then he will provide for the needs of his bride.

Mathew 6 v 33 "but seek first his kingdom and his righteousness and all these things will be added to you as well"

When we seek first the Kingdom of God, then the Lord will add to us everything else that we need as well. I believe that there is also a principle of sowing and reaping that is involved as well. When we give to the Lord, then he will cause a harvest to come back into our lives.

House-hold Salvation

Throughout the word of God, there are so many promises that God has made, not only for us, but also extending to our families as well concerning house-hold salvation and blessing. In Acts 16 we read the story of the Philippian jailer who got saved and then it says in v 33 "immediately, he and all his family were baptised". The man went home and told his family the good news about the gospel and salvation came not only to him but to his whole family. God desires that whole families would be saved. In the Old Testament when the angel of death went throughout the land of Egypt, God instructed the Israelites to stay inside their houses and to put blood around the doorposts, so that the angel of death would pass over them. They were instructed to bring their whole family inside the house in order that they might be saved.

We need to look deep into the word and ask the Lord to show us every promise that he has made for us. In Deuteronomy 28, there is a list of all the blessings that the people of Israel would receive if they walked in God's ways. As we read through the list, we see that there was blessing for every area of their lives that was promised not only for them, but also for their children and future generations. We see listed there, blessing in every area, in their work, in their finances, in their families, in their spiritual lives. God promised that they would be the head and not the tail, that they would have success in all that they put their hand to. What I find so amazing is that, these promises were under the Old Testament covenant and we are told that the New Testament covenant is founded on better promises. Yet, a lot of Christians are not even living in the extent of blessings offered in the Old Testament blessing. Of course, though we have our part to play in living in the blessings. We need to walk in obedience to the Lord and walk in his path ways in order to inherit the blessings that he has purchased for us. If we deliberately walk away from him, then we will forfeit some of the blessings that should have been ours.

Our Ketubah has amazing promises, let's find out what they are and endeavour to walk in them.

The Cup of the Covenant

The next way that the marriage covenant would be sealed, would be by the bride and bridegroom drinking from a cup of the covenant. The bridegroom would pass a cup of wine to his bride in order to seal the contract. She would give her consent to the marriage proposal by drinking from the cup given to her by the bridegroom. However, if she pushed the cup away, then she was rejecting his offer and telling him that she was waiting for someone else. In a marriage there were two cups that were drunk, the first cup would be drunk at the betrothal and the second cup would then be drunk at the final wedding. We see this take on a whole new meaning in the last supper when Jesus sat with his disciples and passed the cup of wine around the table.

Mark 14 v 23 "Then he took the cup, gave thanks and offered it to them and they all drank from it".
Luke 22 v 20 "This cup is the new covenant in my blood, which is shed for you"
Mathew 26 v 29 "I will not drink of this fruit of the vine from now on, until that day when I drink it anew with you in my Father's Kingdom"

Here Jesus was handing the cup of wine to his disciples and he was saying to them - do you accept me as your bridegroom? When we understand the culture and customs of the time, we realise that Jesus was calling his disciples into a covenant of marriage with him and by their acceptance to drink from the cup; they were accepting that covenant with him. He was also saying to them - this is the first cup signifying our betrothal to one another. One day I will drink the second cup with you on that final day of the wedding in my Fathers Kingdom, where we will be fully married to one another. We need to understand that Jesus was speaking about a spiritual union with his people, not an earthly type of marriage.

Every time that we take the cup of communion, we are in fact saying "yes Lord, we accept you as our bridegroom".

The Pharisees and religious people were waiting for someone else, they did not believe that Jesus was the Messiah and accused him of blasphemy in claiming to be God. When we see the significance of some of the things that Jesus did and said, it is hardly surprising that those who did not receive him, got angry with him. Jesus did not fit their profile of how they thought a King should look and be. Jesus was born into this world, in a stable - when they thought a King should be born in a palace. He did not fit their ideal concept of how they thought the Messiah would come. He also mixed with sinners which they did not think he should do and certainly if he was the messiah he would not end up on a cross but would have set up his Kingdom there and then. However, God's ways are not our ways and the Lord chose to visit us in a humble and yet powerful way - how sad that many missed the greatest visitation of their lives. But how many of us often miss God because he does not show up how we imagined he would? Today he is holding out his hands to us, will we accept him?

In light of such an amazing price, how could we reject such a loving bridegroom?

Have we accepted the cup of covenant being offered to us or have we pushed it away because we are waiting for someone else?

<u>Gifts for the Bride</u>

The betrothal also involved the giving of gifts to the bride as well as to her family. The bridegroom would give to his bride something special to remember him while they would be apart waiting for the wedding day. Today we may compare this to an engagement ring given to us.

In a spiritual sense, we have been given many gifts by the Lord while we are waiting for his return to take us home. He has given us forgiveness, righteousness, healing, freedom, peace, love, joy. We have also been given the Holy Spirit to be with us while we wait for the return of the Lord.

John 14 v 26 "But the counsellor the Holy Spirit whom the Father will send in my name, will teach you all things and remind you of everything I have said to you"

The Holy Spirit has been given to us as a deposit guaranteeing what is to come. He will remind us of Jesus and teach us everything that we need to know. The Holy Spirit is the one who teaches us and guides us through this life. He is the one who communicates the will of the Father to us and he is the one who empowers us to fulfil the call of God upon our lives. Jesus said that after he went back to the Father, that he would not leave us alone but would send someone to be with us - the Holy Spirit.

There would also be gifts given to the bride by her father as well, which would be to equip her for her new life a bride. In the same way our heavenly Father has poured out many gifts for us to be able to live our lives as the bride of Christ.

Ephesians 1 v 3 "Who has blessed us with every spiritual blessing in Christ"

We have also been given the gifts of the Holy Spirit, which are to help us to not only be able to live a Christian life, but to be able to fulfil the call of God upon our lives until his return. In 1 Corinthians 12, the bible lists the 9 gifts of the Holy Spirit which are given to believers for the building up of the body of Christ. These gifts are given so that we can encourage one another and so that we can preach the gospel with power and signs following.

We have been given every gift from heaven that there is available, in order for us to be able to live the life that God intends us to live here on earth.

Mikvah

Brides in ancient Israel as well as today may experience a Mikvah prior to their wedding. The word Mikvah means "pool of living water" which is used for purification. Before her wedding a bride would be immersed into the pool of living water, symbolising her purity and the putting off of her old life and starting her new life as a bride. Often the bridegroom would also take a Mikvah. We see that Jesus himself showed us the example of baptism, even though he did not need to be baptised, he showed us the example to follow and he was also following the customs of the day in preparing himself to be the bridegroom. Everything that Jesus did, was pointing towards him being the bridegroom.

Today we see this example in baptism

Mark 16 v 16 "Whoever believes and is baptised will be saved".

When we come to the Lord, we put off our old self and put on the new! If any one is in Christ, he is a new creation. We are to be cleansed daily with the washing of the word. In the Old Testament tabernacle, before the priests could enter into the presence of God, they had to wash in a lava which was in the outer court. We too, need to ask the Lord to cleanse us daily before we enter into the presence of God. Jesus gave another example of washing, when he washed his disciple's feet and told them to do likewise for one another. We may not literally wash ourselves before entering the presence of God, but we need to spiritually ask God to cleanse us on a regular basis. Just as we wash in the natural on a regular basis, so we need to be washed spiritually.

The Betrothal Vow

Once the betrothal had taken place, the bridegroom would then make a promise to the bride concerning the future. This is something awesome that he would have said and again it makes the words that Jesus spoke really come to life and take on a whole new meaning when we understand them in the light of the culture in which they were spoken. The bridegroom would announce to his bride, that he would now return to his father's house and that he would begin to build an extension on the side of his fathers' house which would then become their wedding home. When his father believed that everything was suitable and ready, he would instruct the son to go and get his bride and bring her back to the house.

John 14 v 2 "In my Father's house are many rooms, if it were not so, I would have told you. I go to prepare a place for you. And if I go and prepare a place for you I will come back and take you to be with me that you may also be where I am"

When Jesus spoke these words, he was speaking the words similar to those that a bridegroom would speak to his bride!!

Just as the bridegroom would go back to his fathers house to build a bridal chamber for his new bride, so Jesus has gone back to his fathers' house to prepare a home for us, his bride. Jesus has been spending the last 2,000 years and more building a home for us - we can only imagine how beautiful it will be. God created the world in 7 days and yet he has spent this long on our eternal home.

1 Corinthians 2 v 9 "No eye has seen, no ear has heard, no mind has conceived what God has prepared for those who love him"

If we tried to imagine the most beautiful place that we could think of, if we put together all our greatest dreams and hopes of what our eternal home may look like - our minds are not capable of conceiving it, we can only imagine and not even come close to it.

Revelation 21 v 4 "He will wipe every tear from their eyes. There will be no more death or mourning or pain, for the old order of things has passed away"

One thing that we do know is that in heaven there will be nothing to make us have pain or to ever cry again. That in itself must give us an indication of the beauty that awaits us. There will be no evil in heaven, only holiness - that is why the Lord wants to draw us near to him so that we are prepared for a place of holiness. If we live in darkness and are then suddenly exposed to all consuming light, it will be too much for us to bear, so I believe that is why the Lord wants to prepare his people to live in his light and glory to an extent here on earth now.

John 14 v 3 "I will come back and take you to be with me"

The bridegroom would promise to his bride that when everything was ready, he would come back for her. When Jesus was speaking to his disciples, he assured them that there would come a day when he would return to take them to be with them. Jesus was trying to convey to them the promise of a bridegroom which they should have understood from the culture that they were living in at the time. Obviously the disciples died before the Lord's return, but they would have met the Lord in their death and entered into the place he had prepared for them. There will be two ways that we will meet the Lord - either we will die before his return or we will still be alive at his return. Whichever way, those who have received him, will enter into the place that he has prepared for them.

John 14 v 4 Jesus said "You know the way to the place that I am going" - when the disciples declared that they did not know where he was going, so how could they know the way, he replies to them:

V6 " I am the way and the truth and the life, no-one comes to the Father except through me"

1 Thessalonians 4 v 17 "After that we who are still alive and are left will be caught up together with them in the clouds to meet the Lord in the air"

Jesus has gone to prepare a place for us and one day soon he will return for us to take us to our eternal home to be with him forever.

CHAPTER 2

THE PREPARATION OF THE BRIDE

The Bride waits and makes herself ready

Revelation 19 v 7 "His bride has made herself ready"

Once the bridegroom had made his vow and returned to his fathers' house, the bride had to wait and make herself ready for the return of her bridegroom. Unlike most weddings these days, the bride did not know on what day her bridegroom would return. Most of us if we have been married, knew on what day our wedding would take place, and we prepared ourselves according to that day. In biblical times, the bride did not know on what day her bridegroom would return for her, so she had to wait in a constant state of readiness. She may have had a rough idea of the timing, it would usually be about 12 months that the bridegroom would take to prepare the house, but she would not know the exact day.

I believe that this is where the church is living right now prophetically. We are waiting for the return of our bridegroom, to take us home to live with him in the place that he has prepared for us. We may be getting a sense that the time is closing in because we see the signs around us in the world and we see certain prophecies being fulfilled. However the Bible says that no-one knows the exact hour when the Lord will return.

Mathew 24 v 36 "No-one knows about that day or hour, not even the angels in heaven, nor the Son but only the Father in heaven"

If we have heard people prophesy about the Lord returning on certain dates, then according to the bible they are false prophecies because no man knows the exact time. If God will not reveal it to even angels or the Son, then he will certainly not reveal it to us. We can however get a sense of the timing of the Lord's return and I believe that the Lord does reveal to us as much as he wants us to know and as much as we need to know in order to get ready.

While the bride was waiting, she would wear a veil over her face when she went outside in case any other man decided to offer her a proposal. The veil would show to the world that she was already betrothed. While we do not go around wearing a veil over our face, we are called to be set apart for the Lord. We are in the world but not of the world, there should be something that is different in our life that sets us apart. Most of us if we have been engaged to someone, continued to spend time with them up until the wedding. In our culture it is not normal to get engaged and to then not see someone for a year unless it is for exceptional circumstances such as war, or an army posting etc. I wonder how we would feel if after our engagement, our husband to be announced that he was going away for a year or more to prepare a place for us to stay? I wonder how the bride felt in this situation. It may have been easy for her to wait in the beginning, but after a while it would have been harder, as surely some temptations and even doubts as to whether he would return would creep into her mind. We face these same things as Christians waiting for the return of the Lord. We feel that the Lord is a long time in coming; we may even begin to doubt that he will return and then we begin to give in to other temptations of the world around us. Like the story in the Old Testament where Moses went up the mountain for 40 days, the people began to complain saying "As for this fellow Moses, we don't know what has happened to him". They then proceeded to make a golden calf to worship. When Moses came down from the mountain he was furious and threw the stone tablets with the Ten Commandments on the floor and they smashed. The people had become weary in waiting for Moses and began to worship other gods. In the same way, many have become weary in waiting for the Lord and have given in to other temptations of the world and are not ready for the return of the Lord.

Part of the waiting time would involve purification and it is interesting that in the story of Esther, before she went in to see the King, she was given twelve months of beauty treatments. A year was about the normal time that a bride would have to make preparations before her wedding.

Esther 2 v 12 "Before a girl's turn came to go in to King Xerxes, she had to complete twelve months of beauty treatments prescribed for the women, six months of oil of myrrh and six months with perfumes and cosmetics"

Interestingly, whenever we read of oil in the bible it is referring to the Holy Spirit and the anointing. Esther was soaked in oil for six months in preparation for going to the King and another six months of other perfumes and spices. Part of our preparation to meet the King of Kings is to soak in the anointing of the Holy Spirit who can cleanse us and make us ready for a place in the royal palace.

The first six months of Esther's purification was to be bathed in oil of myrrh. Myrrh was a very expensive ancient oil that was a gum resin from a small shrub like tree and was known for its healing properties. It was used to heal pain before the time of morphine. When Jesus was on the cross he was offered myrrh mixed with wine to ease his pain but he rejected it - Mark 15 v 23. Myrrh was also used to embalm the dead and was sometimes burnt at funerals as well.

John 19 v 39-40 - Nicodemus used myrrh to embalm the body of Jesus after the cross. It was also burnt at times to repel insects.

Myrrh was also used to anoint the doorposts of a bridegroom's house (Song of Songs 5 v 5). It was also used in purification rites and was mentioned as being one of the main ingredients in the anointing oil (exodus 30). In ancient times, a woman's perfume would have been her anointing oil. Myrrh had a bitter taste but a sweet smell and could be associated with repentance. Myrrh was bitter to the taste but produced a sweet aroma to the Lord. Part of the preparation that Esther had to have, was to be cleansed and healed before becoming the King's bride. Right now, the Holy Spirit is cleansing us and healing us so that we are whole to be his bride.

Psalm 45 v 8 "All your garments are scented with myrrh"

The Lord loves sweet smelling aromas. When Esther was preparing to meet the King she sought advice from the King's advisers as to what she should wear and what perfumes to put on etc - in other words, she was finding out what the King liked. We need to find out what pleases the Lord so we can enter into his courts and know his favour.

Signs of the times

Jesus gave us many prophecies of the future so that we would be able to see when the time for his return was getting near. For those who do not know him, it will seem like any normal day when he returns and they will be taken unawares. However for those of us who know him, this day should not surprise us in the same way as we should be seeing the signs and being vigilant and watchful. We are called to be watchmen on the walls, to be a people of prayer and to be a people who understand the times that we are living in.

1 Chronicles 12 v 32 "Men of Issachar understood the times and knew what Israel should do"

We are to be people who understand the times that we are living in, to read the signs that the Lord has given us and know what we are supposed to be doing in these days.

Mathew 16 v 3 "You know how to interpret the appearance of the sky but you can not interpret the signs of the times"

In other words Jesus was saying to the people that they were able to interpret the natural signs in the sky but they could not interpret the spiritual signs from heaven. We ourselves may often look up into the sky at night and say "Red sky at night, shepherds delight" believing that the next day is going to be a nice day. Indeed the Lord in his creation did give us signs in the sky to help us with our lives, especially in the days before modern technology. Often farmers would need to rely upon looking at the signs in the sky to know what the days would be like. However, Jesus was saying - "Why can you not interpret the spiritual signs that I have given to you"?

<u>What are the Signs that we can see?</u>

Mathew 24 lists many things that will begin to take place in the last days, many of these we are already seeing happening right now before our eyes whenever we turn on our television set or pick up a newspaper.

V 6 "You will hear of wars and rumours of wars"
V 7 "Nation will rise against nation, and kingdom against kingdom. There will be earthquakes and famines in various places."
V 8 "All these are the beginning of birth pains"

We have seen wars and conflicts and earthquakes and famines going on for many years, so these in themselves are not the sign of the end, but are the birth pains - as we see these things increasing in intensity and frequency just like a birth, we can know that we are getting nearer to the end that Jesus spoke of.

Luke 21 v 11 "earthquakes, pestilence in various places and fearful events and great signs from heaven"

Every day we are witnessing more and more fearful events and natural disasters.

V20 "When you see Jerusalem being surrounded by armies"

We need to watch what is going on in Israel, as that is a big key to the time of the Lord's return. Israel is God's chosen nation, always has been, always will be and when the armies try to surround Jerusalem then the Lord will return to save his people.

V25 "on the earth nations will be in anguish and perplexity at the roaring and tossing of the sea"

We recently saw the devastations of the tsunami and the havoc that it caused - this could be seen as a prophecy of the tossing of the sea. In England recently we have seen floods across our nation that are highly un-usual for this nation but many lives have been devastated by the floods that have hit our nation this year. We have also experienced freak weather patterns and the changing of our seasons.

V26 "Men will faint with terror"

We see in our nations an increase of terror coming upon people's lives - either from fear of crime, fear of illness, fear of debt etc. Like never before, we live in a society that is consumed by fear as well as the new increased threat of terrorism upon our lives.

V28 "When these things begin to take place, lift up your heads because your redemption is drawing near"

For those who know the Lord as their saviour, it is not a time to be fearful and despairing, but it is a time to get ready because as we see the increase of these signs happening upon the earth, we know that the Lord's return draws near.

Another prophecy that we are seeing fulfilled before our eyes is the return of the Jews to Israel. Over the years the Jewish people have been scattered over the face of the earth, but the Lord promised that in the end times, he would draw them back to their own land in preparation for his return.

Ezekiel 37 v21 "I will take the Israelites out of the nations where they have gone. I will gather them from all around and bring them back into their own land"

Recently many Jewish people have made the trip from many foreign countries back to their homeland of Israel. When the Lord returns he will return to Israel and stand on the Mount of Olives, and he is gathering his people back to the place that he will meet with them.

There are many other prophecies concerning the end times, but we can see from just these few that indeed we are heading towards the day of the Lord. We may not know the exact time, but we do know that we are getting near and that the Lord is calling for his people to wake up from their spiritual slumber and to prepare themselves for his return.

Keeping Oil in our Lamps

Luke 12 v 35 "Be dressed ready for service and keep your lamps burning"

Again, whenever we read of oil in the Bible it is referring to the Holy Spirit - there were lamps in the tabernacle that were to be kept burning day and night before the Lord. We are to be filled with the Holy Spirit on a daily basis, keeping ourselves close to the Lord and awake.

Many because of complacency or discouragement have allowed their lamps to go out, they have not prayed and fellowshipped and re-filled their lamps and their light has gone dim.

The story of the wise and foolish virgins is a parable which highlights the need for readiness and the consequences of not being ready for the Lord's return. The bride would know that her bridegroom was likely to return at night - therefore she would make sure that she was inside the house at night with her lamp and oil ready. As the time of her wedding grew nearer, she would also have in the house with her, her bridesmaids with their lamps ready as well. Everything was ready in case the bridegroom should return that night. I believe that this is a beautiful picture of not only us being ready, but of our responsibility to have all our friends and family ready with us too. The bride would bring all her attendants into the house ready for the bridegroom as well. Just like we read earlier in the story of the Passover, where they had to bring their whole family inside the house, so, those of us who know the Lord have a responsibility to bring our friends and family to know the Lord and to be ready for his return as well.

Mathew 25 v 1-12 tells the story of the ten virgins - five were wise and five were foolish. The five wise virgins took their lamps and a supply of oil with them but the five foolish ones did not take any oil with them.

V5 "The bridegroom was a long time in coming and they all became drowsy and fell asleep"

I believe that this is the place that most of the church is at right now. We have fallen asleep spiritually. Maybe we have heard a lot about the Lord returning, but nothing ever happens, we try to serve the Lord but along the way we have got discouraged and disappointed. We once used to be close to the Lord and pray a lot, but now we have just become complacent and fed up and we have fallen asleep.

2 Peter 3 v 3-4 says that scoffers will come in the last days saying "Where is this coming he promised, ever since our fathers died everything goes on as it has since the beginning of creation.

The Bible actually prophesies that people will mock the second coming of the Lord and not believe that it is actually going to take place.

At midnight the cry went out - " the bridegroom is here, come out to meet him!"

One day the cry will go out and the bridegroom will be here, but will we be ready?

V7 "Then all the virgins woke up and trimmed their lamps. The foolish ones said 'give us some of your oil, our lamps are going out', No, they replied, there may not be enough for both of us"

We can not rely on the faith of someone else; we must keep our own lamps burning and keep ourselves filled with the Holy Spirit. When the Lord returns, we will not be able to rely on the faith of our pastor or our friends; we must have our own relationship with the Lord.

While the foolish virgins were on their way to try to buy some oil, the wise virgins went in to be with the Lord and the door was shut. When the foolish virgins eventually arrived, they found the door shut and when they tried to bang on the door, they were told "I don't know you". There will come a day when the door will be shut and it will be too late. Now is the time that the Lord is calling us and telling us to prepare ourselves.

Making Sure we have our wedding clothes on

Mathew 22 tells the parable of a man who gave a wedding banquet and invited many guests. When the King turned up at the banquet he found a man there who was not wearing wedding clothes;

V12 "Friend, how did you get in here without wedding clothes? The man was speechless

Why was the man speechless? I believe that this story represents the man who thinks that he is saved, but he has never taken off his old life, never put on the new clothes of righteousness that the Lord gives to his people. This could represent the person who has been in church all their life, but never given their life to Jesus, never repented of their sin, never accepted the Lord's righteousness and never really had a change of life. The man was speechless because he thought that he was entitled to be there, but the king commanded that the man be thrown outside because he was not dressed properly.

Isaiah 61 v 10 "For he has clothed me with garments of salvation and arrayed me in a robe of righteousness".

The only garments fitting for the Lord's banquet are the garments of salvation and robes of righteousness, not robes of our own good works.
Revelation 19 v 8 "Fine linen, bright and clean was given her to wear".

We cannot be saved by our good works, but only through the cross of Jesus. I believe that in heaven we may be surprised to see that some people who we thought would be there are not, and some people who we did not think would be there, are there!

Mathew 22 v 14 "For many are invited, but few are chosen"

We looked at the beginning about being chosen and how wonderful that is, but why only a few are chosen when many are invited. I believe that the Lord invites everyone but only a few truly accept him. Therefore the Lord chooses those whom he knows will accept him. The man without his wedding clothes had been invited, but he did not realise that he needed to have a change of heart.

The Warrior Bride - Part of our wedding clothes

Although we are called to be a pure and spotless bride - pure does not mean weak. Jesus never intended his bride to just be floaty and weak and walk around looking pretty. We are also called to be a warrior bride; we have been given power and authority in order to get a job done before the Lord returns.

Acts 1 v7-8 "It is not for you to know the times or dates the Father has set by his own authority but you will receive power when the Holy Spirit comes upon you and you will be my witnesses"

The disciples were questioning the Lord as to whether he was about to establish his Kingdom and he said to them, that they did not need to know when his return or kingdom would be, but they were to just get on with the job in hand and that he would give them power and authority to be able to carry out what he wanted them to do.

We have all been given an assignment from the Lord to be doing while we are waiting for the Lord's return. Waiting does not imply that we are to be sitting with our feet up twiddling our thumbs and singing nice songs! There is a job to be done to prepare the way for the coming of the Lord.

A while ago, I was in a meeting where someone prayed for me and they gave me a picture that the Lord had given them for me. At the time, everyone laughed because it seemed funny, but in fact it is a true picture of what the bride is supposed to look like. The picture was of me in a lovely white wedding dress with army boots on! In a natural wedding you would not wear your lovely dress and then put big clonking boots on! But in Christ it is a perfect picture of who we are supposed to be. We are supposed to be pure and radiant but we are also supposed to be in an army taking ground for the Lord. We are supposed to be moving in power and authority and wielding the sword of the Spirit which is the word of God. Our wedding clothes are both beautiful and powerful at the same time.

2 Corinthians 10 v 4 "The weapons we fight with are not the weapons of the world"

We do not fight as in a natural war; we are fighting a spiritual war against the principalities and powers in the heavenly realms. As such, we have been given spiritual weapons to fight with. We have been given the word of God which is mighty for overcoming the enemy. When Jesus was confronted by the enemy in the wilderness, he overcame by saying "It is written". To be effective in the Lord's army, we need to know what the word of God says about situations and to be able to stand on his promises and declare his word. We have been given the name of Jesus and the blood of Jesus to proclaim the victory of the cross. We have been given the indwelling of the Holy Spirit and all the gifts of the Holy Spirit to help us with what he calls us to do.

Mathew 10 v 16 "I am sending you out among wolves, therefore be as shrewd as snakes and as innocent as doves"

We are called to be innocent but not naïve - pure but not weak. We serve a mighty awesome God and his bride is to reflect that in the earth. We often under estimate the power that is within us. Esther who we looked at earlier, was just one lady chosen to be queen and yet her faith saved a whole nation of Jews. God had strategically placed her in the royal palace for a unique time in history. Esther was a Jew and yet she managed to find herself in the royal palace. God has a way of getting us into the places that he wants us to be for his purposes. When a wicked man called Haman devised a plan to annihilate all the Jews, Esther was in a position to go to the King to beg for mercy on behalf of her people. However, it took courage for Esther to go to the King as she had kept the fact that she herself was a Jew hidden until that time. Sometimes, to step out for God takes courage in many different ways, but her courage was rewarded as she received favour from the King and the plan to annihilate the Jews was over-turned. The faith of one lady impacted a whole nation because she was willing to use the position that God had given to her.

Esther 4 v 14 "Who knows, that you have come to a royal position for such a time as this"

We have all come to a royal position for such a time as this. 1 Peter 2 v 9 says that we are a royal priesthood. Every believer is a part of a royal priesthood and as such we have a powerful position in Christ and can have a great influence in the places that God has placed us to be at this time.

James 5 v 17 "Elijah was a man just like us. He prayed earnestly that it would not rain for three and a half years"

Elijah was a man just like us - in other words, he was human and yet he had a powerful anointing on his life and his prayers were so powerful that they even stopped the rain! When we pray as believers it is powerful, our prayers can change lives and situations. We are called to be a powerful bride not just a pretty bride. We are a bride with a mission, anointed and appointed with a mission and a purpose, we are the warrior bride.

Being found doing what we are supposed to be doing

Another account of the return of the Lord is given in Mathew 24 v36-51
V45 "Who is the faithful and wise servant whom the master has put in charge of the servants in his household to give them their food at the proper time? It will be good for that servant whose master finds him doing so when he returns"

The Lord has assigned responsibilities to each one of us while he is away and we are to be faithful in his work until he returns. When he returns he will want to know if we have accomplished the things that he gave us to do. It will be good for the servant who is found doing what he is supposed to be doing when he returns for he will be rewarded for his faithfulness. However the story also speaks of a servant who becomes weary in doing good and begins to abuse his position of authority and instead of looking after those under him, he begins to treat them badly not thinking that his master will return to see what he is doing.

V50 "The master of that servant will come at an hour when he does not expect"

This illustration often reminds me of an advert that used to be on the television for French polishing. The advert is about a boy whose parents have gone on holiday and while they are away he decides to have a party. He is probably fully intending to clear up the mess before their return but he is caught out as his parents' phone up to say that they have arrived home at the airport early. There then proceeds to be a mad dash to clear up the house and get all the party members to leave as quickly as possible. Just as he thinks he has cleared everything up, he removes something from the coffee table, only to find a huge scratch right across it!! That boy was caught out - he was not doing what he was supposed to be doing and his parents arrived home before he expected them to.

We have been left in charge of different responsibilities on this earth and have been given different gifts and abilities and things to do. Often though we become weary of doing good and we do not believe that the Lord is about to return, sometimes we imagine that he doesn't even know what we are doing anyway. However, the Lord will return like a thief in the night, when we do not expect him.

What would you like to be doing when the Lord returns? Wouldn't it be wonderful to be doing the very thing that the Lord asked us to do rather than doing something that we would be ashamed of? I often think that it would be glorious for the Lord to return just as I was preaching the gospel and people were getting saved and then both I and the new converts would rise to be with the Lord together! What a lovely picture that would be! Could you imagine the surprise on the new converts face - they only gave their life to Jesus 2 minutes ago and now here he is!!

We need to find out what the call of God is upon our lives and begin to fulfil that call.

<u>Our greatest task given to us before the Lord's return</u>

Luke 14 v 15-24 The parable of the great banquet

Jesus gave a parable to illustrate the wedding supper of the Lamb. He spoke of a man who was preparing a banquet and had invited many guests. He sent his servants out to invite the people to come to the banquet, but each one that was invited began to make excuses as to why he couldn't come. In the end the man became angry and told his servants to go out into the roads and country lanes and to make them come in.

Jesus is preparing a banqueting table for us and he is holding out an invitation to anyone who would receive him to come to the banquet that he has prepared. He has also sent us as his servants out into the world to call the people and to invite them to the banquet that he has prepared. However, just like the people in the parable, we find that many people make excuses as to why they can not accept the Lord's invitation to them. One excuse was that they had just bought a field; another excuse was that they had just bought five yoke of oxen and the other made an excuse that they had just got married so they could not come. We can always make excuses as to why we can not accept the Lord or why we can not do his will, but notice that the owner of the house who depicts the Lord did not find these excuses to be valid - he became angry and ordered that the invitation be taken to anyone they could find:- the poor, the crippled, the lame, the blind. Jesus opens wide his invitation to all who would come.

Several years ago, we used to do open air meetings in Ipswich and we would use some puppets for evangelism. We had these cute little puppets that would pretend to sing and dance to different songs and one of the songs was called "Excuses". It goes something like this:- "excuses, excuses, you hear them every day, now the devil he'll supply them, if from church you stay away" It is so true that the devil or even ourselves can come up with lots of excuses not to do the will of God but none of them will stand in the presence of God.

The greatest task that we have been given in these end times is to send out the invitation for all to come to the wedding supper of the Lamb.

V22 "Sir, what you have ordered has been done, but there is still room"

Right up until the coming of the Lord, there will still be room for more to come. I love the words of a song that says "There's room at the cross for you, though many have come, there's still room for one, yes there's room at the cross for you"

So right now we are in a place of waiting for the return of the Lord and we are not to just be sitting idly waiting, but we are to be doing what the Lord has asked us to do. We are also to be seeking to develop a closer relationship with him through prayer, reading the word, fellowshipping with other Christians etc. We are getting ready for a wedding - it should be a time of excitement, expectation and anticipation.

CHAPTER 3

THE BRIDEGROOM RETURNS

After a period of time of waiting, the bride would be rewarded by one day hearing the sound of her bridegroom coming back for her just as he promised. When the wedding house and preparations were completed, the father of the bridegroom would say to his Son "Go get your bride". There is coming a time soon, when the Father will say to the Son "Everything is now ready Son, go get your bride".

When the time was ready for the bridegroom to collect his bride, it would happen in an amazing way. Often the bridegroom would come at night, with his friends and riding on a horse and blowing a Shofar, so that she would know that the bridegroom had arrived. The bride would then be snatched away in the middle of the night just like we will be swept away when the Lord returns. There would be much noise and shouting as they would run through the streets of the night with the wedding procession carrying their lamps.

1 Thessalonians 5 v 2 "The day of the Lord will come like a thief in the night"
1 Thessalonians 4 v 16"For the Lord himself will come down from heaven with a loud command, with the voice of the archangel and with the trumpet call of God|"
1 Thessalonians 4 v 14 "We believe that Jesus died and rose again and so we believe that God will bring with Jesus those who have fallen asleep in him"

When the Lord returns it will not be a quiet affair - it will be noisy and joyful and triumphant. He will come like a thief in the night - not necessarily at night, but the image is of being un-

46

expected to those who are not vigilant and watching for his return. He will come with his friends. He will come with the angels, but he will also bring with him those who have died before us in the Lord. Can you imagine what a glorious day that will be? When, not only will we meet the Lord in the air, but we will also be re-united with those loved ones who have gone before us who knew the Lord. When the bride and bridegroom would arrive at the bridegrooms' father's house, they would find all the other wedding guests already waiting there for them so that they could join in the celebration together when the bride and groom arrived. This is symbolic today of us arriving in heaven and all the people who died before us in the Lord being there waiting for us to celebrate together. I often wonder if this is what is meant by the scripture where it speaks of the great cloud of witnesses in Hebrews 12 v 1. Are some of these witnesses those who have died before us who are cheering us on in this life? And waiting to meet us again? Certainly knowing the Lord is the greatest promise and hope that we have both in this life and in the one to come. Leaving this life is not the end, it is only the beginning. That's why it says:-

1 Thessalonians 4 v 13 "We do not want you to grieve like the rest of men who have no hope".
In Jesus there is hope, even in death, there is life.

A while ago, I had the privilege of being able to preach the gospel at my grandma's funeral. Although I was sad at losing her as I had been very close to her throughout my life, the Lord also gave me an amazing sense of joy in knowing where she was and that she was more than happy, she was the happiest that she had ever been. I had a picture from the Lord of her dancing in heaven and this great sense of joy for her. She had managed to reach her 100th birthday and we had a wonderful birthday celebration with her which was a real gift from the Lord. She died a few months after that, and it was as if she was waiting to reach her

100th as we had often spoken with her about it in the years previous. Although I did not know exactly when she was going to die, the Lord did give me a picture about 2 years before hand of myself preaching in a long white coat at her funeral so I knew that it would be in the winter - which it was. I also knew that when the time came, that I needed to preach at her funeral. I knew that I needed to give her family and friends not only the assurance and comfort that I knew where she was, but I believe that the Lord also wanted the gospel message to be preached. Jesus said "I am the resurrection and the life". I had the privilege of praying with my grandma to receive Jesus into her life when she was about 86 years of age and so as I stood up to preach on that funeral day, I was able to say with total assurance - I KNOW where she is and this is why I know. Jesus said "Whoever believes in me shall never die"

That is also why this passage at the beginning of 1 Thessalonians 4 v13 says that we do not grieve like the rest of men who have no hope. Although death is still sad because we miss those who we loved, it is not without hope. Many times, I have commented to people about the difference between going to a funeral where you know the person was a Christian as opposed to a funeral where you were not sure if they were or not. In one place there is hope and the other place only despair and emptiness. The hope that we have is that not only will the Lord return for us, but he will bring with him those who have fallen asleep in him before us - what a party awaits!!

A poor example might be when you have not seen someone for a long time and you go to visit them on a long flight and as you come through the security arrivals gate at the airport, you scan the crowds and then you see them! As you embrace, you are overwhelmed with your excitement at seeing those who you have not seen for so long. In heaven, there is a great welcoming committee waiting for us to usher us into the presence of God.

Luke 21 v 27 "At that time they will see the Son of Man coming in a cloud with power and great glory"

There is coming a day soon when we will see the Son of Man coming in great power and glory riding on the clouds with the armies of heaven following him in great procession blowing trumpets and shouting "Arise my bride, Come away with me"

Song of Songs 2 v 13 "Arise, come, my darling; my beautiful one, come with me"

The Wedding would take place

The wedding ceremony would now take place under a huppah which was a like a canopy and was often made out of an outstretched tallit which is a Jewish prayer shawl. A prayer shawl has fringes on the end of it that look like wings. This was symbolic of the bridegroom taking his wife under the shelter of his wings into his protection and under his authority. The Lord takes us under the shelter of his wings and offers us protection as we hide in him.

Psalm 36 v 7 "Both high and low among men, find refuge in the shadow of your wings"
Psalm 57 v 1 "I will take refuge in the shadow of your wings until disaster has passed"
Psalm 61 v 4 "I long to dwell in your tent for ever and take refuge in the shelter of your wings"

A canopy would have been like a tent. We can see from the Old Testament that many things are a shadow of the promises to come. The Israelites used to worship in a tabernacle which was like a large tent and we then see in Revelation 21 v 3 "Now the tabernacle of God is with men and he will dwell with them" The man made tabernacle of the Old Testament was just a shadow of the true bridal tabernacle - the wedding canopy where we will truly enter into the Holy of Holies and know the glory of God forever.

The bride and bridegroom would enter into the bridal chamber that the bridegroom had prepared and would honeymoon there for 7 days before coming out for the final wedding supper to take place. This speaks of a place of intimacy and as we enter into the holy of holies, we enter into a place of spiritual intimacy with the Lord. It is symbolic of when the church will be lifted up from off the earth to be with the Lord and we will spend 7 years with the Lord while the great tribulation is being poured out on the earth. While the earth is experiencing the worst time in all history, those who have received the Lord will be having a spiritual honeymoon in the Fathers house.

Romans 6 v 5 "We will certainly also be united with him in his resurrection"
Isaiah 26 v 20 "Go my people, enter your rooms and shut the door behind you; hide yourselves for a little while until his wrath has passed by"

The Lord will hide us in the bridal chamber, while his wrath is being poured out upon the rest of the earth. We shall be hidden in his hiding place, the secret place - known only to the bride.

In the parable of the wise and foolish virgins, the ones who did not bring their oil were too late and the door was SHUT! God will gather his people into the huppah and the door will be shut. It will be too late at that point for those on earth who suddenly realise that indeed Jesus is who he said he was, to change their minds. They will have to go through the time of tribulation about to be poured out. Now is the time of grace and mercy, now is the time that the Lord is giving us to respond to his invitation.

Revelation 7 v 14 "These are they who have come out of the great tribulation, they have washed their robes and made them white in the blood of the lamb"

V15 "Therefore they are before the throne of God and serve him day and night in his temple; and he who sits on the throne will spread his tent over them"

The Lord will spread his bridal canopy over his people and hide them from the coming judgement. I believe that in light of these and many other consistent scriptures in the word of God, that the bride will be taken out of the world before the tribulation takes place. The tribulation is God pouring out his wrath upon the earth for the evil that they have done in forsaking him. Therefore God does not judge his own chosen bride with the rebellious. Throughout biblical history we see that God always took his people out of the way before judgement was poured out.

Why I believe the church must go before the tribulation

2 Thessalonians 2 v 7 "For the secret power of lawlessness is already at work; but the one who now holds it back will continue to do so until he is taken out of the way and then the lawless one will be revealed whom the Lord Jesus will overthrow with the breath of his mouth and destroy by the splendour of his coming"

I believe that this verse is speaking about the evil that we see operating in the world today but it is held back in some respects from operating fully because of the existence of the Holy Spirit and bride of Christ being on the earth. When the church is raptured, the Holy Spirit will depart with the bride. At that time there will be an un-leashing of evil in an unprecedented way that has never been seen before. At the moment there are prayers of the saints going up before the Lord for the earth and situations that we see around us, but when that is removed, there will be terror. In ancient times, the servant would go to find the bride and would then return back to the Son at his Father's house with the bride. The Holy Spirit has been sent to earth to draw us to Jesus, but once the bride is fully gathered in and ready, he will depart with us to return to the Son in the Father's house.

Why I believe that the church will leave the earth before the tribulation is also because God does not judge the righteous with the un-righteous. It has never been in his nature to do so and he does not change.

1 Thessalonians 5 v 9 "For God did not appoint us to suffer wrath but to receive salvation through our Lord Jesus Christ, so that whether we are awake or asleep we may live together with him"

In Genesis 6 we see the historical story of Noah and the flood. God was grieved that he had made man because of his wicked ways and he decided that he would send a flood to wipe out all mankind. However Noah found favour in the eyes of the Lord and God instructed him to build an ark so that he and his family would be saved during the time of the flood. God wanted to preserve the good of mankind and begin again with Noah and his family. This was the first example of how God did not judge the righteous with the un-righteous, but gave him a way to be saved.

1 Peter 3 v 20 "When God waited patiently in the days of Noah while the ark was being built. In it only a few people eight in all were saved through water. This water now symbolises baptism that saves you also"

God waited patiently holding back his judgement until Noah had completed the ark. During that time, Noah would have been preaching to the people who asked him why he was building an ark telling them to repent of the coming wrath of God. It would seem though that no-one listened to him, as the scripture says only 8 people were saved through going into the ark. Today the ark is Jesus who we run into for our salvation and the water that the ark went through is the baptism.

After the flood God made a promise with mankind that he would never again flood the earth and he said that the rainbow in the sky would be a sign of his covenant. Every time it rains and afterwards you look up in the sky - that is the promise of God all these years later. What an awesome covenant keeping God we serve!

2 Peter 3 v 9 "The Lord is not slow in keeping his promise, as some understand slowness. He is patient with us, not wanting anyone to perish, but everyone to come to repentance"

Maybe we have often wondered why the Lord is delaying his return, why is he so long in coming? Maybe it is because he is waiting and waiting the longest possible time because he wants more and more people to be saved and to be a part of his bride. He desires that none would be lost. If the Lord had returned a few years ago, maybe some of you reading this now would not have made it??

In Genesis 18 the Lord is again angry because of the wickedness of the people in Sodom and Gomorrah and he confides in Abraham that he is going to destroy them. Abraham pleads on behalf of the people and the Lord tells him that if he can find just ten righteous people in the land, then he will spare the whole place. Sadly ten righteous people can not be found and God is about to destroy the place. However before he is able to destroy it, there is a relative of Abraham's called Lot who was living in Sodom and an angel is sent there to warn Lot to leave that place because the wrath of God is coming.

Genesis 19 v 14 "Hurry and get out of this place because the Lord is about to destroy the city"
V22 "Flee there quickly, because I can not do anything until you reach it"
V29 "So when God destroyed the cities of the plain, he remembered Abraham and brought Lot out of the catastrophe that overthrew the cities where Lot had lived"

The Lord did not destroy the city until Lot had left. Notice that the angel said that he could not do anything until Lot had left the city. I therefore believe that if we are to look at the consistent nature and character of God throughout scripture, we can see that he always removes his people before his judgement. Therefore I believe that before God pours out his wrath of the tribulation, that the church must leave the earth. However we have a choice to walk with the Lord or to decide to stay under judgement. Lot's wife had the opportunity to escape judgement and yet she hankered after her old life in the sinful city and began to look back and as she did so, she was turned into a pillar of salt. If we want to walk in the ways of the world, in our old life, then we could end up being judged with the world too.

Genesis 19 v 26 "Lot's wife looked back and she became a pillar of salt"

<u>The wedding supper will take place</u>

Once the 7 days had passed, the bride and groom would come out from the bridal chamber and the wedding supper would take place. The bride would no longer be wearing her veil, as she was now seen to all as the wife of the bridegroom. Right now, the gospel is veiled to those who are perishing, but one day all will see who the Lord is and who his bride is.

Revelation 19 v 7 "Let us rejoice and be glad and give him glory, for the wedding supper of the lamb has come and the bride has made herself ready"

V9 "Blessed are those who are invited to the wedding supper of the lamb"

There will be great rejoicing and dancing just like in a Jewish wedding, where there would be much exuberant partying. Anyone who thinks that heaven will be quiet, may be in for a shock. Anyone who thinks that you should not dance in church, will also be surprised to see that heaven is full of dancing and joy. It will be a time of great celebration and how can we be sad at such a glorious time.

Song of Songs 2 v 4 "He has taken me to the banqueting hall and his banner over me is love"
Isaiah 25 v 6 "on this mountain, the Lord Almighty will prepare a feast of rich food for all peoples, a banquet of aged wine - the best of meats and the finest of wines"
V8 "The Lord will wipe away the tears from all faces"

We can only imagine what the wedding supper will be like. Definitely heaven is real and we are going to have new glorified bodies and we are going to be able to experience emotions of joy and we are going to be able to eat food. When Jesus was raised from the dead and he appeared to his disciples on the beach, he ate fish with them. He was in his glorified body and yet he was able to eat.

When I was younger, I used to have a strange idea of heaven, maybe like a lot of people do. I imagined that in heaven you just floated around on clouds and it was all very fairy tale like! The bible however gives a completely different picture of heaven.

Heaven is a real place, where we will have new glorified bodies that will never age or decay ever again. We will live in mansions that the Lord has prepared for us. A while back, I had a picture in my mind of what I believed heaven to look like. As I was praying I saw a beautiful grassy field with a slope going down towards a river with a tree standing at the bottom. I imagine heaven to be so bright and alive, where even the flowers seem to be alive and almost talk to you as you walk along. Indeed the bible does speak of creation groaning waiting for the redemption day; even flowers will not die in heaven. Nothing can die in heaven, for the Lord is total life. A few weeks after I had seen this picture, I was out shopping and went into a charity shop and saw a picture hanging on the wall for sale. When I looked at the picture it was almost identical to the image of heaven that I had seen when I had been praying previously. I was amazed that the Lord was confirming that what I had seen was true. I bought the picture and it now hangs on the dining room wall. I believe that deep down inside each one of us is the child like innocence that has been given to us from the Lord. As children we enjoyed maybe watching Disney films where the animals talked and nature seemed to be alive. We imagined that place "Somewhere over the rainbow"! Even as adults these kinds of films can capture the child within us and we long for such a beautiful place but often think that it is just a fantasy. However, I believe that the reason that we long for these kinds of things, is because that is part of what our real home will look like. Some people have differing views of whether animals will be in heaven - but I believe that they will be because they are part of God's creation. They have a will, emotions etc and their own characters and they are special to the Lord as well as to us. The Bible even speaks about trees clapping their hands and stones praising God! All of creation will be alive and will praise God in heaven - what a wonderful place that will be.

Heaven will be a place that is full of pure light and pure love -

there will be no need for any fear in heaven. Imagine being able to walk anywhere you like at any time without fear of any harm. There will also be no cost; Jesus already paid the price for our eternal home. No more nasty bills through your door in heaven! Jesus said "come and drink freely". All that we need will be provided.

I believe that we will also have responsibilities given to us according to how faithful we have been with what he asked us to do here. I believe that heaven is how earth was intended to be before we messed it up. Man was never created to die. I believe that is why we find death so hard to understand, because we were never created to die. It was only sin that caused us to become mortal. At the cross, Jesus took our sin and purchased back for us eternal life. We will have to die in this earth so that we can get rid of this mortal body and put on a new immortal body which can house us forever. The real YOU, the spirit within your body will never die. Our new body will be a perfect body that can never die again or ever get sick or have pains! Hallelujah!

At the wedding supper we will eat all kinds of things which maybe we have never even heard of before. It will also be a time where we will be able to meet all kinds of interesting people. What would you like to ask Moses for example? Or maybe David or Elijah? Just imagine being able to speak to the old prophets or the New Testament apostles and hearing their stories firsthand, as well as catching up with all our old friends and family. I think that we will also be amazed at what we will find out in heaven as well. It may be that we will have people coming up to us in the streets of heaven and saying "Thank you, I am here because of you". Some of them may have been people who we knew that we led to the Lord, but others we may not even know them and yet for some reason we touched their lives without even knowing it". Maybe someone was in a meeting where we preached or even overheard a conversation we were having with someone else on a bus and it led them to think about Jesus. Every little seed that we sow for the Kingdom of God in this life will never be wasted and we may never realise the extent of it until one day. Let us remember that in this life, the only things that will last for eternity are those things which we do for the Kingdom of God.

After the wedding supper, the bride and groom would then live their lives together as husband and wife. In the same way, we will dwell with the Lord forever.

Psalm 23 v 6 "And I will dwell in the house of the Lord forever"

Revelation 21 v 2 "I saw the holy city, the new Jerusalem coming down out of heaven, prepared as a bride beautifully dressed for her husband"

After the 7 years of tribulation, there will be great rejoicing as the Lord establishes his Kingdom and he will rule and reign victorious with his bride by his side.

Revelation 21 v 2 "Now the dwelling of God is with men and he will live with them"

The greatest thing about heaven is that we will live with God without any barrier between us. God created us for relationship with him - one day it will be completely restored. Right now he is calling us closer in preparation of that final day!

SUMMARY

We can see that by understanding the old customs and Jewish traditions, that many of the things that Jesus did and said were pointing to him being our bridegroom. The people of the day would have understood the significance of the things that he taught and did. When we get a clear revelation and understanding, we are amazed at the meaning for us.

Jesus himself came as a Jew and as such lived by a lot of the Jewish customs. In explaining to his people who he was, he would have kept to the ways that they would have been able to understand. Sadly, today we do not have the same understanding and so often a lot of treasures in scripture are lost.

So to conclude at a glance:-

The Father would choose a bride for his son	The Father chose us for his Son
Either the Son or the servant would go to Draw the bride	Jesus came himself but also The Holy Spirit is now here Still drawing the bride
A bride price would be paid	Jesus paid the highest price
A betrothal covenant would be made	He gave us his word
The Bride must accept	Our choice
A cup would be drunk	The communion
Gifts would be given to the bride from The bridegroom and her father	We have been given spiritual Gifts
A Mitvah would take place	Baptism

A vow would be given	Jesus promised us a place
The bridegroom would depart	Jesus has gone to prepare the wedding home for us
He would promise to return	Jesus said he will return for us
The bride waits and prepares herself	We are waiting now
The bridegroom would return	Anytime soon
Bride and groom taken to the huppah	7 years with the Lord during The tribulation
The wedding supper of the Lamb	Glorious hope to come

Women Arise Ministries

I hope that you have been blessed by this book. Women Arise is a Christian ministry that holds various women's conferences to encourage and teach women how to arise into their potential in Christ. If you would like further information about this ministry, please visit our website - www.womenariseministries.net